Anthony

THE POETRY FIELD

AUSTIN MACAULEY PUBLISHERS™
LONDON • CAMBRIDGE • NEW YORK • SHARJAH

Copyright © Anthony Keyes 2024

The right of Anthony Keyes to be identified as author of this work has been asserted by the author in accordance with sections 77 and 78 of the Copyright, Designs and Patents Act 1988.

All rights reserved. No part of this publication may be reproduced, stored in a retrieval system, or transmitted in any form or by any means, electronic, mechanical, photocopying, recording, or otherwise, without the prior permission of the publishers.

Any person who commits any unauthorised act in relation to this publication may be liable to criminal prosecution and civil claims for damages.

A CIP catalogue record for this title is available from the British Library.

ISBN 9781035841080 (Paperback)
ISBN 9781035841097 (ePub e-book)

www.austinmacauley.com

First Published 2024
Austin Macauley Publishers Ltd®
1 Canada Square
Canary Wharf
London
E14 5AA

Acknowledgements

Many thanks go to the following people:
Stewart, Demi, Darren, Joe, Phil, Josh, Emily, Carmel, Liz, Gary, Toby, Kelvin, Richard, James, Neil, Rob, Andy, Jo and Bridget.

For the community with affection and thanks to:
Birnbeck Regeneration Trust
Uphill Village Society
National Trust Sand Point and Middle Hope
Worlebury St Paul's School
The Former W-s-M Miniature Railway (Bob's train)
North Somerset Council
Weston Town Council
Weston Mercury
BBC Radio Somerset
BBC Radio Bristol
The Bristol Post
Western Daily Press.
Worle Community School Academy

Front cover photograph by the author.
A rainbow pictured in a tree beside the lake at Puxton Park, Hewish, Weston-super-Mare.

Back cover photograph by the author.
Waverley paddle steamer passing the Old Church of St Nicholas, Uphill, Weston-super-Mare.
The church is pictured on the horizon.

Table of Contents

Go	9
The Calm See!	10
Peregrine Falcon	11
I Wander, I Wonder.	12
Soul Mates	13
Devotion	14
Icelandic Saga	15
Godspeed	16
Cents and Sensibility	17
Remembrance	18
Scarlet Silence	21
Sincerely Yours	22
Shell Shock	23
Standing By	24
New Life, New Life.	25
Friends to the End	26
The Ki-ing's Road	27
Inspired	29
Heart Beat	30
Train of Thought	31
The Tunnel of Life	33
Longton Grove Road	34
Out of Spirits	35
Bow to Experience	36
Waiting Ages	37
Shadows	38
Mindfulness	39
Rainbow Kiss	40
Antiquity	41
A Poet's Dream	42
Moonshot	43

Conversation	44
The Old Crooked House	45
Seashells	46
Acquiring Signal	47
Calming Wings	48
The Cliff Face	49
The Art of Sound	50
Time Out	51
The North Somerset Seashore Poetry Trail	52
Trail Plaque Locations	53
Posset	56
Wave Back	57
Midnight Music	58
Lighting Strike	59
Beatles Rock Intro	60
Beatles Rock	61
Time Storm Cove	64
A Mirror for the Clouds	66
The Plaza Principle	67
Seashore	68
SON ET LUMIÈRE	70
SON ET LUMIÈRE (Adapted)	71
Funny Moments	73

Author's Note

The following poems by Anthony Keyes were featured in part in the author's previous book titled *Poetic Realms* including the *Weston-super-Mare Seashore Trail*, published 1999. Five of these poems are now included to form the completed North Somerset Seashore Poetry Trail, a physical poetry plaque trail you can visit and place yourself in the poem settings and discover new poems along the way.

Anthony's new exciting full trail of eleven poems now features for the first time in this book as the North Somerset Seashore Poetry Trail.

- Midnight Music
- Time Storm Cove
- A Mirror for the Clouds
- The Tidal Trail (Seashore)
- SON ET LUMIÈRE

Introduction

Imagine yourself in the poem settings within this book.

Visit some or all of the poems' spectacular landscapes.

Eleven of Anthony's West Country poems have been engraved upon plaques. All set in their exciting poetic locations and blended with nature.

Discover the new North Somerset Seashore Poetry Trail covering Portishead Clevedon, and Weston-Super-Mare.

The Weston section of the route covers approximately five km each way from Uphill Nature Reserve and Uphill, Weston Seafront, The Town Square, Marine Lake, Anchor Head Cove, and onto the poem titled *Beatles Rock,* which is placed upon the sea wall overlooking Birnbeck Pier Weston. Going further then you may wish to venture on north of Weston to Sand Point and Middie Hope and discover the two poem settings in this beautiful National Trust area.

Look out for the poem titled "Wave Back" which can be found set upon Clevedon's splendid seafront promenade near to the bandstand.

At Portishead on the seafront, you will find the poem titled "Posset" the name used in medieval times by the locals for Portishead.

You can visit these locations for free and join the trail at any point, take the book with you. Enjoy wonderful views along the coastal footpath north of Clevedon Pier and visit Ladye Bay, then on to Portishead.

There are many more new poems unrelated to the Seashore Poetry Trail waiting to be discovered from cover to cover in this spiritual book.

Anthony's poems have been featured live and recorded on TV, radio, magazines, newspapers, and broadcast live on the internet as well as in more than fifty different poetry anthology books.

The Poetry Field is Anthony's long awaited and acclaimed original illustrated poetry book:

Go

Go and put your shoes on.
They will take you far.
Be who are you.

The Calm See!

Stay calm.

Do not be alarmed.

If you lose your head,

You cannot see,

To where it is,

You want to be.

Peregrine Falcon

Try a skeleton key
To unlock what maybe.
Drifting slowly,
Slowly as swans on a lake.
Our feet guide us to the beat.
Together, unique.
No sound beneath.
Will the Eye of Horus reveal
How we should feel.

I Wander, I Wonder.

I wonder.

If you are not here.

If you are not there

I wander, I wonder.

Left quiet, left to ponder.

A frozen teardrop halts a new frontier.

Beyond space and time,

Thinking around,

Lost in the crowd.

A flowing flux as pebbles move underfoot.

The scream of the storm.

As the Phoenix breaks before Dawn.

Looking up at the ice kite.

The fright, the flight, the emptiness,

Gone from the night.

Soul Mates

My past family tree,
Has departed from me.
My tears fall down
To the roots.

Drops of water to the vine
To nourish the divine.
Opening my mind to the folks,
Waiting in a family line.

I shed new life
With my breath.

Evaporating sad feelings.
Remembering names.
Believing in those who remain.

Devotion

Grandeur from the shore.
A big new ship to explore.
An ocean, fear and commotion.
Cherished final emotions.

God was with them,
Even more so that night.
Never to waver, together.
Last looks, tight hugs, goodbye.

Mr and Mrs Louch of Weston.
1912 the prime of their lives.
Charles, a life preserver.
A kiss into the lifeboat for Alice.

A single return.
Memories are now eternal.
Two hearts, one home.
Home is Edelweiss.

Icelandic Saga

Intense lunar space heating.
Supplied by lunate water plume greetings.
The rendezvous, a planned meeting?
I shiver by the glass frozen river.

Charmed upon a carpet of moonlight.
Following a succession of sparkling
Diamonds into the night.
Silvery blue tones of fresh light.

I channel the boiling core.
Burning as loud as a lion's roar.
The small hidden people are a suggestion.
Are they real? Is the question.

Amid a deluge of boulder shores.
Are tiny brightly painted square doors.
They signal entry,
Into the unseen world.

The small hidden people, watching.
From the other side.
Hiding in a fine place.
So fine, no human will find it!

Godspeed

We are all
Part of the past.
We are all
Part of the now.
We are all
Part of the future.

Our loved ones
Are always with us.
You are never alone.
There is a plan.

Cents and Sensibility

There is a woman singing in the underpass,
Her song touches me, singing aloud so fast.

"Do you have two cents?" she asked.

Love is a sense.
Do we all have common sense?
A second sight.
Maybe even sixth.

There is a woman singing in the underpass.
I wonder for her as I pass.

It is a Bear Pit hit,
Do you have one dime
Or will you walk pass this time?

"Do you have two cents?" she asked!

There is a woman singing in the underpass,
I wonder how long her song will last?

Remembrance

The Weston-Super-Mare Remembrance Day Service was held in Grove Park Weston at 11am on 11 November 2018 marking the passing of 100 years since the end of World War I. The guns on the Western Front fell silent at 11am on 11 November 1918 when the Armistice was signed.

The band led a parade of Royal British Legion members, Cadet forces, Scouts and Guides to the park at 10.25 am. In the park there were screens to stream the commemoration live on YouTube.

It started at 10.50 am with a poem written and performed by Anthony Keyes titled "Scarlet Silence".

During the reading, there was silence from the crowd that filled the park and those who watched outside on the screens.

In the background the bird song of the park could be heard.

Toby Mitchell then 16 years of age played Anthony's great-uncle Herbert Fenton Byrne's restored violin which had only been played once before at Worlebury St Paul's School Remembrance Service 13 November 2014, this being the first time since Herbert himself last played it before the outbreak of World War I, July 28, 1914. Herbert died in the Battle of the Somme in July 1916 and is buried in France.

There were approximately 415 Guides and Scouts gathered around the war memorial to represent the names engraved upon it. The Guide and Scout leaders then planted 25 crosses inscribed with the names of the different conflicts that had taken place between World War I and the present day in which Allied soldiers have lost their lives.

The public were welcomed after the service had ended to plant their own crosses in the Field of Remembrance in front of the War Memorial in the park.

THE DAY

It was a morning that was meant to be, the rain clouds parted, sunshine, right on cue appeared.

The music played on Herbert's violin with its original bow was witnessed in person between 3,000 to 4,000 people that gathered in and around Grove Park.

It was the largest attendance ever, as people paid their respects to all affected by war and conflict.

Herbert's violin sung out to a now silent park, you could hear the leaves moving on the trees, the bird song of the park was in tune as Toby Mitchell played the piece by the composer Ralph Vaughan Williams.

The musical work of 1914 titled "The Lark Ascending".

It was scored by Williams for a solo violin and piano and revised by the composer for a solo violin and orchestra in 1920.

Pictured on 13/11/14.

A canvas by Anthony Keyes of the poet's great uncle, H.F.B.

This original canvas was placed on a music stand to mark the first occasion of Herbert's restored violin being played during a school Remembrance Service. 'Bertie' himself was the last person to play his violin almost 100 years before.

Herbert Fenton Byrne.
Private 14015 'Bristol's Own' 'A' Company
12th Battalion Gloucestershire Regiment.
1914/15 Star and The British and Victory Medals.
Died of wounds in 'The Battle of the Somme' July 1916.
Founder member of the Battalion Band.
A renowned violinist with a rich bass voice.

Pte Herbert Byrne

Sunday 11th November 2018.

"The crowd in unison fell quiet in private contemplation and all that could be heard above the haunting tones of the violin solo, was the plaintive sound of birdsong as if in instinctive accompaniment."

Gary Hawks.
Parade Commander.

Scarlet Silence

Give thanks to remember,
The fallen's last breath.

Give thanks to remember,
After their death.

Give thanks to remember,
Your memory our guide.

Give thanks to remember,
Be at their side.

Sincerely Yours

There were millions of me.
That fought for thee.
Keeping you free.

We cannot borrow,
From your tomorrow.
Your freedom cost us dearly.

So clearly, forget us not.
For when you pause,
We will always be,

Sincerely yours.

Shell Shock

Crash another wave.
Just like the one, goodbye.
Where am I now?

A cry out loud sigh.
I dive for cover, thinking of my lover.
Where is my mother?

Will I be gone this day?

My friends,
My friends,
My friends,

So is this my end…

Standing By

The experience.
All shot up.
Why did you not turn back?
"Why the thought never occurred to me."
Another day in the "office".

Beyond brave,
At the ready, to beat the grave.
The airborne cost so high,
The lucky few return to the deck.
Kites in the clouds.
Trusty steeds circling like gnats.

Altitude to freedom.
"My luck was in
This time!"
Sighs of relief.
Another thumps up,
A wave of the hand over the head, "Open up".

Memories of friends, good chaps.
Who were there for our tomorrows.
Our tomorrows are their brave remembrance.
"Message received and understood."

New Life, New Life.

Through the strife,
Seeking a better life.
So much more to explore.
So much more,
Than we knew before.

A shared day in every way.
Feelings of well-being,
Leading to a new beginning.

The past faded,
A smile raised at the passing,
Dancing butterflies.

At the dawn of the birds' song,
We become one of the heavenly choir.
It is for us to enquire.

Friends to the End

Created on this island rock,
That time forgot.
Above a breathless
Gripping sea.

The memory of Campbell paddle
Steamers now bereft.
There is little left to see.

Defiant hands of fate.
A new combination to reopen the long
Locked gates.

Kept afloat with a tightrope and
The might of the lifeboat.

An open canvas to the shore.
The new old proud pier to beckon
Once more.

A fine sight.
Take your seats,
The pier show is about to start.

Birnbeck Pier and Island

The Ki-ing's Road

A swagger and sway,
Home and away,
His Stamford Bridge way.

Now standing nine feet high.
The Shed End, battle cry.
Born is the King, Osgood.

The King of The Blue's.
With kit so true.
Peter played without fear.

A diving header,
A real goal getter.
A shot so fast.

Memories that last.
Kneeling in the net,
No one can forget.

A share in the cups.
Fulfilling dreams.
Part of a great team.

Imagine today.
The flight of the ball
The emotion of it all.

Number 9 on his back.
The Statue, Chelsea.
Ossie is back.

Peter Osgood. "Ossie".

Inspired

April showers, 2021.
See the flowers
In the rain.
"Opening up again."

No longer tight shut.
Watch the buds open up.
Sunshine to last,
When the petals scatter,
No matter.
Fade away the pain,
Just like flowers in rain.

Heart Beat

There was a time of elation.
A creation of who we used to be.
Memories for you and me.

Visions of you come to mind.
We went to and fro.
Only for fate to let us go.

Train of Thought

Singing, rumbling tracks.
Last call for the 2012 diesel haul.
Maybe the steam train bliss.

For a short memory mile,
Feet on the boards,
Remember the gathering hoards.
Hold on tight, even watch that kite.

The children's tram,
Adults run up and down.
Putting on the green,
Leaving you lean.

Seagulls resting on the lawns,
Applauding opening yawns.
Waiting for the passing train.
Except in the rain.

Now having putted the tees.
Time for a quiet morning tea.
Until, alert bells ring.
Hear the toot, toot sing.
Wild waving, now another craving.

Special memory souvenirs.
Through the Years.
Forward to platform 2023.
A place to rest and enjoy
Amongst "SEEMONSTER" foliage.
A four season's ticket.
Follow the line of enquiry.

The former 820 metre, 7¼ gauge Weston-Super-Mare Miniature Railway opened in 1981 on Weston's Marine Parade seafront beach lawns.
Bob and Sue Bullock took it over in 1983 and ran it until it closed during September 2012.
Josh is pictured in the driving seat with the engine turned off (16.09.12) while "Dylan" prepares to depart for one of the last journeys.
During 2023 an exciting planted repurposed area was constructed and is called "SEEMONSTER GARDEN".

The Tunnel of Life

Eyes fixed firmly ahead.
Legs feel like lead.
Passing intermittent flashes of light.
Thinking of life's turning points.
Looking back with a sudden,
Turning of the head.

How far have I come?
What is left to come?
The light is bright,
Drawing me on.
Trying to do what is right.
I move ahead.

The mellow birds serenade the path.
A robin drops down to the ground.
Stares, flies off suddenly.
Straining my eyes far into the distance.
Knowing we all go to sleep in the end.
Who waits at the exit gates?

My feet skip in time,
Along the bird song chorus line.
Foliage bushes brushing against me.
Time flowing ever faster.
A forthcoming "SPRIT"! awaits.
I know "I" was missing!

Longton Grove Road

This front door we saw.

Throughout the years

The shadows fall,

Some walked tall.

In the hour of need.

Ghosts of the families past.

A door of NO.

A door of YES.

We can only guest.

Two World Wars.

A bomb or two

Flew down the chimney breast.

It came to rest and burnt a child's,

New dress.

Behind this blue panel door

This house kept safe, families all,

But to you it's just an opening door.

Out of Spirits

A ghost you say!

Because you may,

Think you have nobody.

Let your spirit

Sing within.

Use your energy

In other ways.

You will be amazed.

At your spirits

External gaze.

Bow to Experience

Waterline dry, landlocked high.
Stays and fans spinning.
Tapping wind in the rigging.
A boom swaying, a bowsprit.

A stern named, "Marooned".
All hands needed on land.
Imagine, full sail ahead.
No broken glass or holes in the hull.

Exquisite as an art exhibit.
Needing a lick, now derelict.
Forgotten, left and rotten.
Berthed upon the earth.

Waiting Ages

Forward time travel.
A day return.
Boarding aged 16.
Mind the gap.
Ever so keen.
Run down the lane
To the forward fast train.

Upgraded on board.
Classed as an adult.
Clickety-clack, clickety-clack,
Mind the gap, mind the gap.
On your way back.
Take yourself with you.
Aha, still aged 16.
Disembark, now time
To play in the park.

Shadows

Walk tall,

Your shadows will follow.

Look not at others.

Reflect upon yourself.

A life full of meaning.

Your equity defining

Your equality.

Equal responsibility

Resourcing your mind

Empowerment to find.

Mindfulness

The reality of a distant memory.
Returning to a place you knew well.
In time with space, you face.
It is exactly as it used to be.

Fine detail you thought you forgot.
Then time passes for now.
Returning, returning again,
The distance of memory becomes today.

Rainbow Kiss

A Rainbow came my way.
Moving like a swing bridge.
Stepping within,
I saw the beginning.
I saw the end.

A rainbow carpet.
A simple heart fit.
The blessing of the skies
To stop passers-by.

Mighty colours of
Changing light.
Who knows when
I might see the living
Daylights again.

Antiquity

A stone with a start date.
An icicle to the heart date,
Time to depart date.

Now the end date,
The waiting at heaven's
Gate date.

Now the questions?

What did you do
In-between dates.

A Poet's Dream

Here is a thought.
When we are gone,
Our words linger on.

Feelings in print,
As long as we think.
All that is left is the ink.

Then we blink.
Close our eyes,
To rest in eternal lullabies.

A word for the now,
Tomorrow it reads.

As we grow older,
We cannot hide,
From the incoming tide.

Memories to discover,
From this side of the curtain.

Of that we are certain.

Moonshot

Remembering 1969.
A long ago time.
Looking at that glowing moon.
Thinking without blinking,
Some people are up there
Looking back at me.

As I walk on this planet,
Made of basalt and granite.
I see far away
Basalt deposits and
Regolith soil.

Evidence of many impact events,
But none more stunning,
Than the impact of people walking
On the surface of the moon.

Conversation

Passing strangers
Leaving half heard
Conversations,
Lingering in the air.

Joining up the
Chit chat chatter.
Make new words.
Sentences that matter.

A fresh meaning.
An interview at the point
Of reception,
Now that is perception!

The Old Crooked House

I carefully open the ancient,
Sticking wooden crooked door.
In this converted crooked building.

A crooked pleasant waiting room.
I sit in the crooked comfort seat.
Squinting at the old crooked walls,
Before that wonderful picture falls.

I ponder at the crooked mirror.
Would you straighten it?
Or just leave it as it is.
In the old crooked house.

Seashells

Shilly shally
Dilly dally
Shilly shally
Dilly dally.

Wobbling willy nilly
On the moving shingles
Upon the surely shore.

Acquiring Signal

Seconds out.

Scanning recognition.

Where does the time go?

To and fro,

Passing through time,

We once knew.

So here we are,

Both near and far.

Signal acquired.

Wait one minute,

What am I doing tomorrow!

Calming Wings

Heavens above

With calming wings,

A feather floating in the breeze.

An angel's embrace,

Just in case.

For all the human race.

From the summer to the fall.

The angels guarding all.

Parish Church of St Mary, Christon.

The memorial window depicting Sergeant Kenneth Durrant killed in action during WW2. The window is dedicated to his family.

The Cliff Face

Smooth soaring shapes.
Passing this way and that.
Gliding over a steep overhanging
Worn and crumbling cliff edge.

Looking up the only option.
Let your heart raise up to the magic
Of nature looking to the beyond.
Surging feelings to new heights.

The Art of Sound

The creatives,

Colour me.

The sound of song

A heartbeat for so long.

Pulse beats of impressions,

Imprints that leave the expression.

Like shadows on glass.

Time Out

A stratosphere from the heavens.
The rhyme of time.
Passing as a Kaleidoscope.
Mingling our ways.

Rising and setting days,
That pass us by in a haze.
Transparent thoughts,
Gone with the blink of an eye.

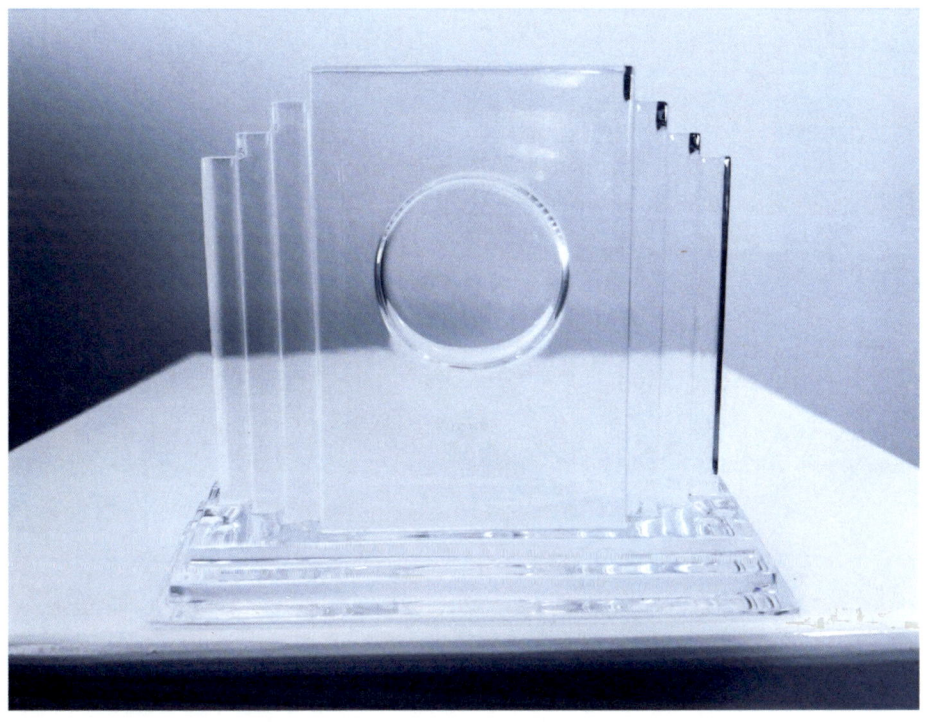

The North Somerset Seashore Poetry Trail

Trail Plaque Locations

North Somerset Seashore Poetry Plaque Trail. Portishead, Clevedon and Weston-super-Mare.

Portishead. "Posset" Seafront promenade on the low wall by the concrete bench near the Open Air Pool.

Clevedon. "Wave Back".
Green Beach Clevedon Seafront.
Near the bandstand on the stone wall by the bench. On route to Ladye Bay.

Middle Hope. "Midnight Music".
National Trust. Sand Point on the path wall at start of the footpath leading to Middle Hope.

Sand Point. "Lighting Strike". National Trust. Sand Point on the path wall at the start of the footpath leading to Sand Point.

By Birnbeck Pier.
"Beatles Rock"
On the sea wall coping stone overlooking Birnbeck Pier and Beatles Rock.

Anchor Head
"Time Storm Cove"
Poem extract.
On the sea wall, left hand side by the steps leading down to Anchor Head Cove beach.

Marine Lake
"A Mirror For The Clouds"
On the stone wall beside the former Knightstone Theatre building by the steps leading to and from the Marine Lake.

Town Square
"The Plaza Principle"
Town Square wall by the ground level water fountains.

Weston Seafront
"Seashore"
Placed on the sea wall of the viewing across the Channel map to Wales.

Uphill Hill Local Nature Reserve
"SON ET LUMIÉRE"
Situated at the bottom of the hill on the stone wall, on the path leading to and from the Old Church St Nicholas Uphill, adjacent to the main road off Uphill Way.

Uphill Hill Old Church St Nicholas.
Adapted version of "SON ET LUMIÈRE" at the top of the Uphill hill on the stone wall by the church kissing gate leading to and from Local Nature Reserve.

****

Plaque map information correct at time of publication. There are various styles to look out for including Modern, Victorian, Art Deco, Edwardian and Mediaeval designs.

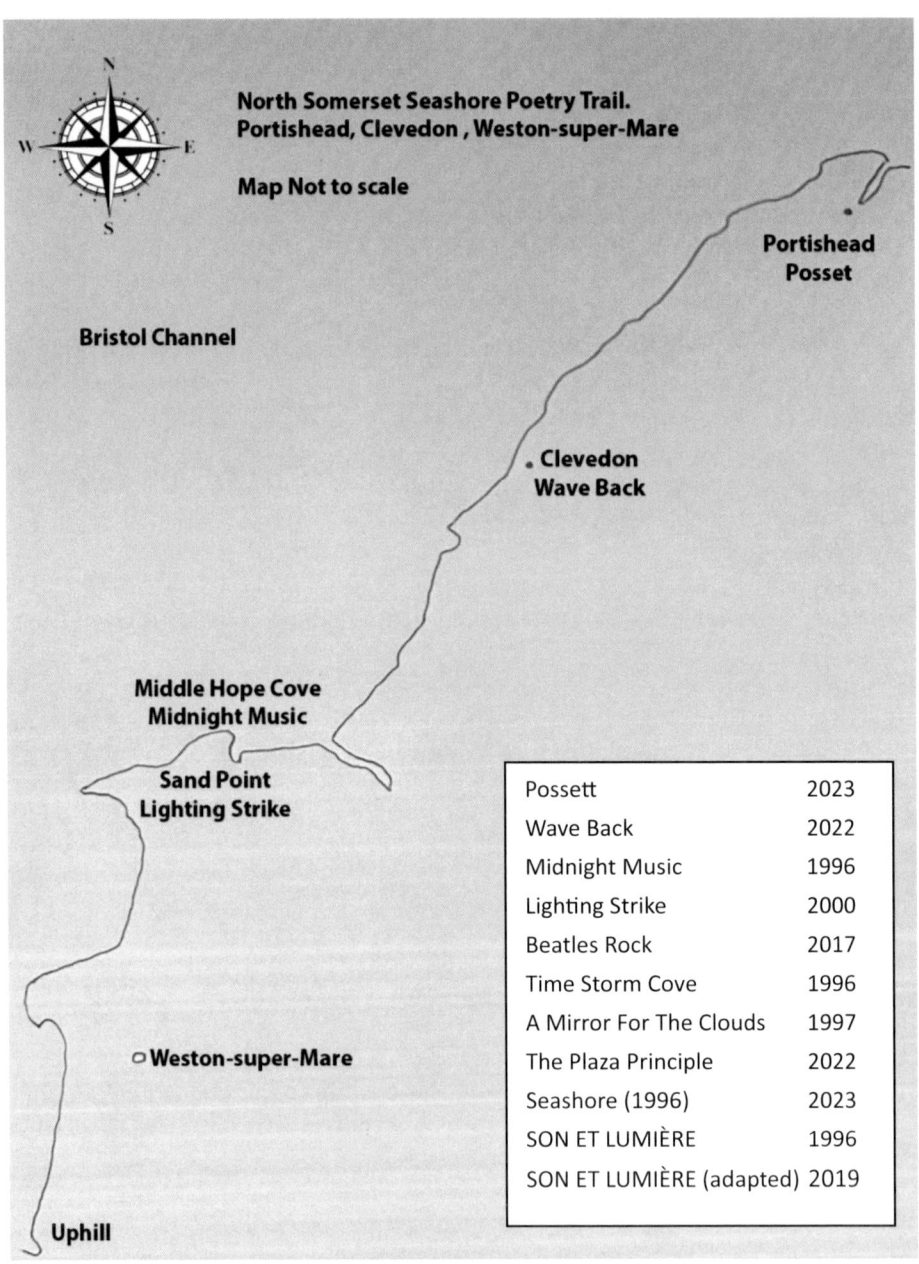

Weston-super-Mare, Section of North Somerset Seashore Poetry Plaque Trail

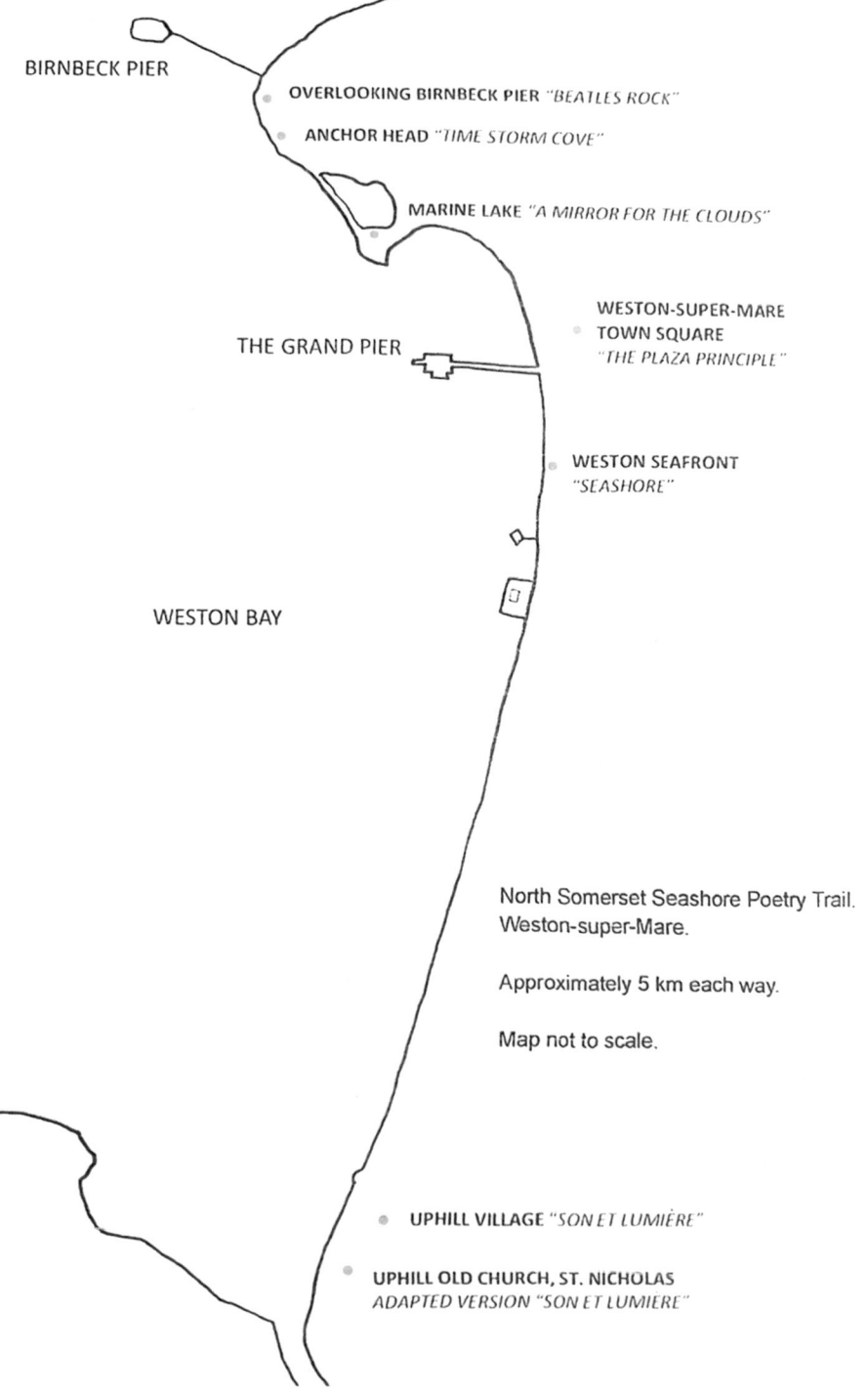

Posset

Portishead, North Somerset

Wave Back

Upon Ladye Bay
The sea's spray
Refreshed my face.
I "waved" to the sea.
A sudden misty embrace
Partly obscured the
Ghostly magnificence
That is Clevedon Pier.

Ladye Bay Clevedon is a short walk north of Clevedon Pier.
The coastal footpath also runs between Portishead and Clevedon.

Midnight Music

Rock pool footprints unfold
As an accordion.
Blending in harmony with the landscape.
Mesmerising high cirrus clouds await
A returning current.

Rhapsody wind crescendos shiver the senses,
Performing a sea spray melody.
Lyrically the night chills to cold.
Slippery seaweed hugs part submerged
Boulders protecting a divers drift overture.

Wave compositions serenade Middle Hope
Cove as the full-blooded sun descends to
Silence, a lullaby sunset flashes vivid colours
To sleep.

Grey moon pebbles, roll as sea shanty songs,
While waning disco lights ripen to blackness.
The blustery midnight blue notes wash away
Recollection.
Grass like violin strings cut through the hearts
Logic.

Dark green walks embrace the purple thistles,
Upon sloping lyceum sea fields.
Revealing their epistles to a minstrel
Symphony of dreams and desires for our
Hearts to aspire.

Middle Hope.

Lighting Strike

Ode to a long kiss of life.
Eternal waves impact this rock
As I run upon the vital green
That cloaks Sand Point.

A white lighting strike.
Stops me in its path.
A thunderclap to catch me
In its trap.

I step back to the brink
Only to think!
Swift were the thoughts,
That follow me.

Sand Point.
A panoramic perspective of changing light.

Beatles Rock Intro

The Title of the poem is in the poem.

A permanent reminder of the week spent in Weston-super-Mare by one of the soon to be most famous bands in world.

The Beatles performed at the Weston Odeon for one week in July 1963, staying at the now demolished Royal Pier Hotel near Birnbeck Pier.

The group had a publicity photograph taken showing Paul McCartney, John Lennon, Ringo Starr and George Harrison sitting together on a rock with Birnbeck Pier used as a backdrop.

That photograph location has now been immortalised with the "Beatles Rock" poem written on a granite stone plaque which is embedded into the seawall coping stone.

The poem "Beatles Rock" overlooks that same rock that was used by The Beatles in the famous 1963 photograph.

Sixty years later in 2023 the art deco Odeon cinema where The Beatles performed closed. The original stage on which The Beatles performed was still in place. Merlin Cinemas reopened the cinema 15-12-23. It was renamed Plaza Cinema.

Pictured 'Beatles Rock'

Beatles Rock

The rock which The Beatles were pictured upon.

1912 P&A Campbell Ltd, an original Timetable of Sailings

Waverley, the world's last seagoing paddle steamer.
Bristol Channel, Weston, June 7th 2023.

Time Storm Cove

Tilting of an antique clock,
Unexpectedly time stops.
Serenity brings forth forgotten thoughts,
Like falling rain from blue sky.
Past times reflecting a straight connection
With the future.

Our Ancestors, built ornamental walk-ways
In the sky to keep their feet dry.
Breezy seaspray memories cometh forth,
The war like onslaught of splendid paddle
Steamers.

Today mere dancing shadows preside at the
Old Pier side.
No more melodramatic induced clanks on
Smooth wooden planks.
The grandeur of dusky sepia postcards,
Capturing a faded haze for all to be amazed.

Exhilarated, sat the workers, high and low
On boulder ledges pondering amidst
Impregnable orange sun glints of quirky
Craggy rocks.
Refreshed, rested voyagers posed a tranquil
Picture.

Yet no time for a smile,
Relaxation lasts a short while.
Jubilant and serene, the glittering sunlit
Slipway, part submerged, moisten by
Wallowing sea brine.

Songs of white waters wash,
Assimilating over worn cliff-stones,
Oblivious to traces of yesterday's diminishing
Footsteps at Anchor Head Cove.

All at sea on this present day,
The splash, the dash of waves carrying
Ye olde clandestine voices, capture with each
Rapture and roar as though names of half
Heard conversation with spirits of sweeping skies.

Pause not, as the jaded stranger shuffles
Past, asking, "Have you got the right time?"
Suffice to say, the right time is now,
It's all around you.

A Mirror for the Clouds

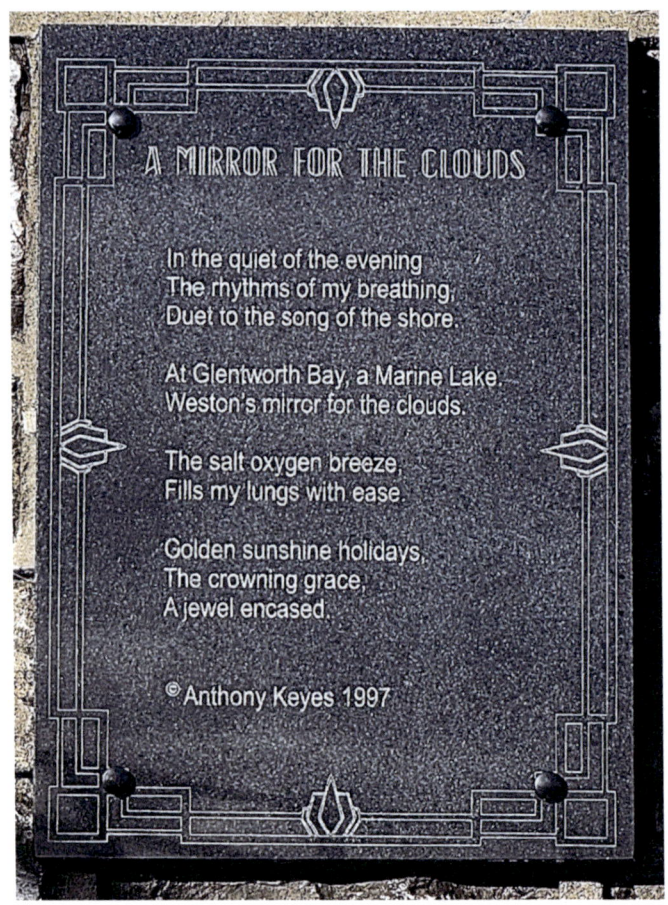

The Plaza Principle

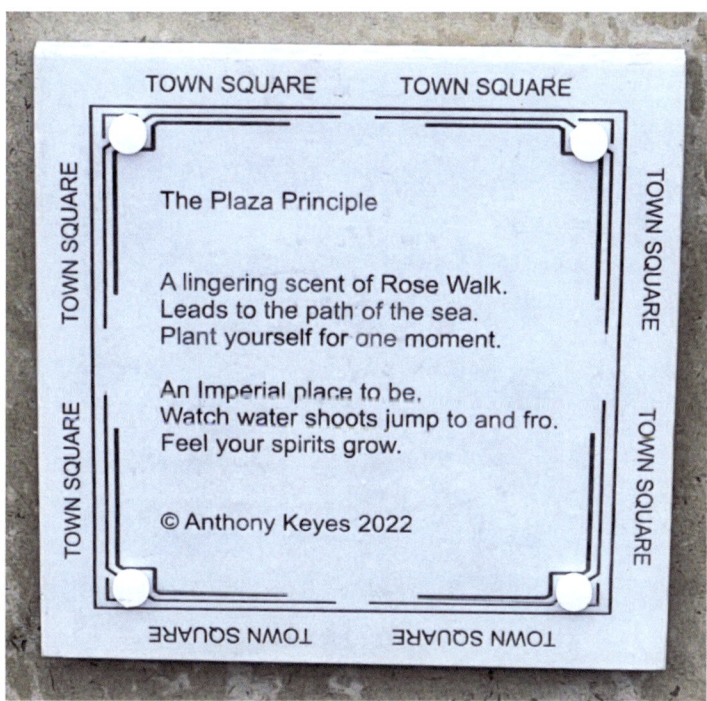

Seashore

I thought I saw you there,
In the sunshine of Weston-super-Mare.
Following the Seashore Poetry Trail.
Walking to marvellous places,
Clevedon, Portishead seasonal graces.
North Somerset jubilant, serene, seafront.
Strolling peaceful promenade romances.
Happy sea song acknowledging glances.
Sundance glares, Royal Parade's fine air.

I thought I saw your golden light.
In the breaking waves of the Weston night.
Rhythms of the sea, sing it back to me.
The natural harmony, the spring, the fall
A poetic North Somerset trail for all.

Use a mirror to read the poem plaque and reflected extract on Weston seafront. "Seashore" has been amended from the author's originally titled poem "The Tidal Trail".

SON ET LUMIÈRE

England's petite nautical Norman church, St Nicholas.
A high altar apex oasis, green Uphill downs
Sound swept by howling savanna winds.
Wondrous panoramic views, fluttering chalkhill blues.
A time out of time, sweet aromatic thyme.
Dark Viking hours, treading on yellow rock rose,
From the flame, to the crest;
The returning rambling robin constructs her nest.

Seafaring limestone pavement floor, exulting standing tall.
The spirit of the seas, the swashbuckling Weston breeze.
Nature's propellant pulse, ascending a marine shell sorrow,
Nay, the morrow embraces thick round twig hedges
Spaced in abandonment, like a lonely glacier lake
Awaiting the caressing dance of Easter's green wake.

SON ET LUMIÈRE (Adapted)

The local flora and fauna have been highlighted with capitals in the adapted poem by the poet so that the words stand out for the reader.

The reflection of the church can be seen on the plaque in the picture.

SON ET LUMIÈRE was adapted by the author in 2019 into an eight-line version in granite stone.

This plaque is situated next to one of the kissing gates that leads from The Old St Nicholas Church at Uphill to Uphill Tower.

Uphill Hill and Uphill Local Nature Reserve are situated south of the village of Uphill and south of Weston-super-Mare.

A site of Special Scientific Interest and a Special Area of Conversation.

The full sonnet poem "SON ET LUMIÈRE" plaque can be found on the stone wall near the foot of the path leading to the Old Church St Nicolas off Uphill way.